Old HILLFOOTS
MENSTRIE, ALVA, TILLICOULTRY and I

by
Guthrie Hutton

The Hillfoots boasted many large mansion houses, with extensive grounds requiring the services of gardeners such as these photographed by McCallum & McDougall of Duke Street, Alva.

First Published in the United Kingdom, 2003
by Stenlake Publishing
Telephone / Fax 01290 551122

ISBN 1 84033 242 5

The publishers regret that they cannot supply
copies of any pictures featured in this book.

ACKNOWLEDGEMENTS
I am indebted to Bob and Barbara McCutcheon, Eric Eunson,
Alan Geddes, Dollar Academy archives and Dollar Museum for
permission to use pictures in this book. It would not have been
possible without their help and co-operation.

SOME FURTHER READING
The books listed below were used by the author during his
research. With the exception of the last three, none are available
from Stenlake Publishing, and anyone interested in finding out
more is advised to contact their local bookshop or library.

Clackmannan Libraries have produced a number of excellent
local publications including:

Adamson, John, *Menstrie, A People's History*, 1996
Cowper, A.S., *Sidelights on Alva History*, 1983
Lothian, James, *Alloa and its Environs*, 1861, reprinted 1983
Ure, Adrian, *Local Railways*, Volumes 1 and 2, 1986/87
   Other titles referred to were:
Baillie, Bruce, *History of Dollar*, 1998
Day, J.P., *The Counties of Clackmannan and Kinross*, 1915
Evans, Eric J., *Tillicoultry, A Centenary History 1871–1971*, 1972
Gibson, William, *Reminiscences of Dollar, Tillicoultry & etc.*, 1882
Murray, Ian, *The Hillfoots in Old Picture Postcards*, 1995
Swan, Adam, *Clackmannan and the Ochils: An Illustrated Guide*,
   1987
The Dollar Magazine (various issues)
   Also by Guthrie Hutton for Stenlake Publishing:
*Mining from Kirkintilloch to Clackmannan and Stirling to
   Slamannan* ISBN 1 84033 132 1
Old Alloa ISBN 1 84033 223 9
*Old Clackmannan, Sauchie, Tullibody and other airts of the Wee
   County* ISBN 1 84033 238 7

WHAT and WHERE are the HILLFOOTS ?
The Hillfoots' only definite boundary is the base of the Ochil Hills to the north,
although the River Devon forms an equally natural southern line. To the east and
west, however, the limits are debatable and so for the purposes of this book I have
kept within the old Clackmannanshire borders – those that existed when I was a boy
– with Menstrie to the west and Dollar to the east. I hope that your enjoyment of this
book will not be spoiled if you disagree with this definition!

The old Hillfoots road passing through old Menstrie.

MENSTRIE

With hills to graze sheep on and fast-running burns to provide power to drive mills, the Hillfoots were (excuse the pun) tailor-made for the woollen industry. Added to these natural advantages, a growing population in the towns and cities of the central belt provided a ready market for the mills' finished goods. The first of Menstrie's large mills was established in 1800, setting a trend that was to shape not just Menstrie but the other Hillfoots towns too.

The new turnpike road also helped to influence the way the Hillfoots developed (a turnpike road was a toll road named after the barrier which was turned to allow a vehicle to pass after the toll had been paid). This was made around 1806 to replace the old Hillfoots road which clung to the lower slopes of the hills, following their every contour and undulation. The new road was everything the old one was not. It was broad, straight and well-surfaced, and it ran across the flat ground to the south of the hills. Over time the towns and villages of the Hillfoots also shifted south and grew along the new road, as if they were new communities.

Menstrie was the exception because the old and new roads remained close together where they crossed the burn, which helped to keep the village more unified and compact. As the population grew along with the mills in the nineteenth century, buildings filled the space between the two roads and spread along the new road matching the existing development beside the old one. Much of the old road still survives between Menstrie and Alva despite having been superseded long ago.

Water Woes

The hills and burns may have helped the Hillfoots to achieve a measure of prosperity, but there was a downside too. Confined watercourses pouring off such high and extensive catchment areas were prone to flooding. On one level, the sight of turbulent, muddy water roaring off the hills accompanied by the sound of unseen rocks rolling and crashing beneath the surface was exhilarating. More seriously the flooding burns were dangerous and occasionally resulted in drownings. They also damaged buildings and killed sheep. None of the Hillfoots towns and villages escaped the floods and all have tales to tell. In October 1822 Menstrie burn was swollen from heavy rain when some girls met on a plank being used as a temporary bridge. Too afraid to pass or turn back, they became giddy and fell in. The older girls were able to save themselves, but the smallest was carried about 40 yards before a young man, attracted to the incident by the screams, came to her rescue.

Now known as Ochil Road, the old or 'back' road is seen here crossing Menstrie's 'auld brig' which dates from 1665.

Menstrie Glen   Valentine's Series

Just upstream from Menstrie bridge was a meal mill dating from the mid-seventeenth century. A remnant of its burnside wall can still be seen although the site is now occupied by a Scout hall. A wooden dam, seen in the picture above, was wedged across the burn to provide a head of water to drive the mill. The water was taken off along a wooden trough which carried it over the wheel, but instead of simply pouring off the end and driving the wheel clockwise, the wooden hopper, seen in the picture on the right, turned it back on itself and rotated the wheel anti-clockwise. The water was then collected at the base of the wheel and fed along another wooden trough to drive a mill further downstream.

The trough taking the used water from the meal mill's wheel to a mill on the south side of the main road can be seen to the right, suspended over the burn. In this early twentieth century picture the burnside is a hive of activity, with small works of various kinds on either side. They have now been replaced with housing, a medical centre and a small park. The houses in the background are built along the old road – the large three-storey one on the left was known as Windsor Castle. Its origins are unclear and the name may just have been a local nickname because it was a lot bigger than any of the neighbouring cottages, but it was apparently occupied by the influential Holbourne family before they acquired Menstrie Castle and they may have used it as a dower house for the castle. It was certainly a fine example of Scottish vernacular architecture, which makes its demolition by the council in the 1950s regrettable to say the least!

Menstrie and its mills grew in size and stature through the nineteenth century, as this picture from around 1890 shows. The large mill in the right background was Drummond & Johnston's Elmbank Mills which dated from the 1860s, and although the buildings have now gone the Elmbank name survives as a business centre. Drummond & Johnston also built houses across the road from the mills and their stone-carved initials can be seen above the door of cottages dating from 1872. The same interwoven D & J initials appear on one of three carved stone plaques between the first floor windows of an adjacent two-storey building called Ochil Place, completed in 1873. Unlike these initials the partnership was not cast in stone and, after a quarrel, Johnston bought Drummond out and continued to operate the mills himself until the end of the century. His own mansion house, Broomhall, was a wee bit grander than the smaller millside dwellings.

The background of any view looking west along Menstrie's Main Street is almost bound to include Dumyat, the distinctive hill at the west end of the Ochils. In the foreground here, on the left, is the co-op with the Parish Church just beyond. Menstrie was originally part of Logie Parish and village folk had to walk the two miles to worship at Logie Kirk until a chapel of ease, seen in the background of the picture on the previous page, was opened in 1880. Menstrie was later transferred to Alva Parish and the chapel of ease elevated to the status of Parish Church following a bequest from the last of the Holbourne family, which also paid for the enlargement of the church and the building of a manse and hall. The co-op also had a hall on the first floor of its store. The Menstrie Co-operative Society was in existence for just over 100 years before amalgamating with Alloa's co-op. The large clock above the central first floor window was installed in 1897 to mark the society's silver jubilee.

Menstrie's early development had been largely based on the fortunes of its castle and estate. William Alexander of Menstrie Castle was one of King James VI's most trusted aides. He was knighted in 1609 and as the King's principal Secretary of State for Scotland was given the job of founding the colony of Nova Scotia. When the scheme was abandoned five years later the monies promised to Sir William were never paid and he died, in debt, in 1640. The sixteenth century castle and estate were sold to Sir James Holbourne and in 1719 to Alexander Abercromby, but when his family disposed of them decline set in, until, by the time this picture of the courtyard was taken around 1900, the castle was in a bad way. It continued to decay and in the early 1950s there were calls for its demolition and even schemes to rebuild it in Nova Scotia. It was saved when an appeal was set up in 1957 inspired by campaigners, actor Moultrie Kelsall and local man John Drysdale. The building, restored as council flats and surrounded by new council housing, was visited by the Queen on 28 June 1968.

Before Menstrie, Alva, Tillicoultry and Dollar took on their present shapes there were a number of small hamlets dotted along the base of the hills. This one, entitled Damsburn on this early twentieth century postcard, was to the east of Menstrie and must have been typical of these small farming communities, known in the old Scots tongue as 'fermtouns'. Some of them were absorbed into the growing towns and villages, some disappeared, and one or two, like this one, managed to retain a semblance of identity while becoming part of their larger neighbours. The little burn that passes to the east of these buildings runs on towards Glenochil Distillery, Menstrie's industrial survivor, continuing a tradition that started in the early eighteenth century. Myretoun House, a small mansion that took its name from the hill behind these houses, stood just to the east of them.

ALVA

Like Menstrie, Alva's development was built on the fortunes of its woollen mills, but it also enjoyed some patronage from the lairds of Alva House. Sir John Erskine wanted to create a planned burgh using some of the great wealth he had amassed from his silver mines in Silver Glen. These yielded Britain's biggest ever find of what was also a very pure silver ore, but Sir John backed the wrong side in the 1715 Jacobite rebellion and although he was eventually allowed to return from exile he was never rich again. His work of developing the burgh was continued by John Johnstone who bought the estate in 1775. He was from a landed Lanarkshire family and had made his money as a soldier (of fortune) in India. Alva House remained in the possession of the Johnstone family up to the death in 1929 of the kindly, benevolent but fiscally imprudent Miss Carrie Johnstone. The contents of the house and estate were sold after her death but failed to match her debts. The house, which had started out as a sixteenth century tower house and been extended with an impressive south facade in 1820, did not sell. It was allowed to fall into disrepair and was used for artillery target practice during the Second World War.

Weaving on hand looms was already established in Alva at the start of the nineteenth century when the first water-driven woollen mill was set up, but large-scale development was inhibited by the poor flow in the burn. That changed when James Raymond Johnstone inherited the estate from his father John. In the 1820s he developed the burn's potential by clearing rock that was stifling the flow of water and building a dam from which lades were run to power mills.

Later in the nineteenth century, mills began to be set up on sites away from the burn as coal-fired steam power took over from water power, but Alva was also proud of generating another source of energy from coal: gas. The gasworks in Henry Street was thought to supply the cheapest gas in Scotland. It was originally set up by the Alva Gas Company and in 1878 was bought by the town council. In the 1930s the works was taken over again, this time by Alloa Town Council which operated it in association with their larger gasworks.

Water Woes

Floods affected Alva too although the exact location of an incident that took place in the summer of 1832 is difficult to deduce from a dramatic contemporary account. It describes a waterspout bursting over the Ochils, inundating Alva and sweeping the Stirling to Perth mail coach into the flooded River Devon – quite a sweep unless the writer was being economical with accuracy when interpreting the location. There were apparently no passengers and the driver and guard managed to scramble to safety, but the horses were trapped and although one did free itself they both drowned. A lad named David Moir managed to salvage most of the mail and was given a £5 reward by the postmaster general.

The upper end of Alva Glen showing the zig-zag road which eased the gradient and made the final hike to the top just a little less strenuous.

ZIG ZAG ROAD, ALVA GLEN.

ILLUMINATIONS IN ALVA   A 7858

Alva Glen was clearly regarded as a place of many attractions. Despite this, the publisher of the postcard on the right has sought to enhance its appeal by sticking the picture of the couple locked in a fond embrace onto the photograph of the bridge. The couple appear on postcards of local beauty spots from all over the country – computers may do it better, but picture enhancement is as old as photography itself! The use of light to enhance buildings and places at night is also a well-tried idea as Alva's autumn illuminations show. The annual display, seen here in a picture from the mid-1930s, attracted thousands of people who came by the busload to see the remarkable spectacle of the glen with its waterfalls and strategically placed stuffed animals lit up by coloured lights.

James, son of James Raymond Johnstone, gifted Johnstone Park to the burgh which formally accepted it at a ceremony in 1856. The park, to the west of the town, was the venue for the annual Alva Games and other special events like the celebration of royal occasions. These were frequent between 1897 and 1911, beginning with Queen Victoria's Diamond Jubilee, followed by her funeral, Edward VII's coronation, his funeral and culminating in the coronation of King George V. Alva folk were clearly not suffering from celebration fatigue by June 1911 when they gathered at Johnstone Park in their hundreds to mark George V's crowning. The houses in the background are in Beauclerc Street which, along with Back Road to the west of Carnaughton Burn, continues the line of the old Hillfoots road across the top of Alva. The street takes its name from Lady Frederick Beauclerc, the married name of James Raymond Johnstone's daughter Jemima. Behind the houses is the golf course, opened in 1901, where sheep, untroubled by all the goings-on at the park, keep the rough well mown.

Alva's park land was extended in 1923 by the addition of Cochrane Park adjoining Johnstone Park to the west. It was gifted to the burgh by three brothers: James, John and Charles Cochrane, descendants of an Alva family which emigrated to America in the 1860s and, no doubt using skills acquired back home, prospered making woollen shawls. The brothers also gifted Cochrane Hall which took over from the old town hall as the main meeting hall for the town when it opened at the park entrance gates in 1930. The park has changed little over the years although the children's maypole and roundabout have been replaced by some more adventurous apparatus. In the background to the left is the wall of Listerlea house and in the centre is Dalmore School with the old public baths and wash-houses behind. To the right is the Glentana Mills, now a visitor centre for the Hillfoots Mill Trail, and behind it is Coblecrook Mill.

Home of Rest, Alva

Oh! there's a hame in Alva that's unco dear to me,
  It rests my weary soul and charms my restless e'e.
It nestles 'neath the hills, yet stands serene and bricht
  Wi' poplar trees ayont, and the Johnstone Park in sicht.

The young forgether there in the happy simmer time,
  The Silver Glen they view, and the Ochil Hills they climb.
When they return leg weary they rest wi' little care,
  For this hame provides a' comforts that ilka ane may share.

Resting in the prophet's chamber, the sunlight streaming in,
  Or erstwhile, the verandah, wi' fragrant flooers abune,
Then to hear the gong asounding, and to settle doon and dine,
  Oh! it's fine to be a leddy – for a month – in simmer time.

Some ithers gang in autumn or winter there to stay,
  For oft they're sad and weary, wi the burden o' the day;
But when at hame in Alva they rest wi' min' content,
  For peace and plenty there abound, and ease for those forspent.

Sae mony o' us weemen, sair trauchled nicht and day,
  Sometimes forget we hae a soul, and seldom do we pray.
But there at hame in Alva, 'tis brocht back to oor min'
  By her wha leads us back to God, and things forgot lang syne.

So it's hame, hame, hame, and hame fain wad I be,
  And hear the birdies singing aroon the apple tree;
To see the beauteous garden and to hear that kindly voice,
  These hamely sichts and soonds, I ween, wad gar my hert rejoice.

The Lady Aberdeen Memorial Home, at the western end of Beauclerc Street, was a holiday hostel for the Scottish Girls' Friendly Society, an organisation dedicated to the welfare of domestic maids. As ever there was a Johnstone behind it – Miss Carrie – who inherited Alva estate in 1888. She would have been well acquainted with the needs of maids as at one time her own family employed nineteen servants of various kinds. The building now faces the war memorial – a reminder of the awful event that sparked the process of social change that hastened the demise of domestic service. But for the girls who stayed there, the home was also a haven:

Domestic service was not confined to the large mansions of the super-rich; often people living in relatively modest circumstances would employ a maid to carry out household chores like cleaning, washing and setting the fires. It is difficult to be sure if the young woman standing at the gate of this house in Alva was a maid or one of the family, but she was certainly doing domestic chores. The picture was used as a postcard in 1908 and in the message on the back she complains that it 'was the washing day I got this taken [and] I had not time to put on my other garb'. It was sent to her sister, care of a Dr John Gray in North Kelvinside, Glasgow, a part of the city where many professional people lived and who would almost invariably employ domestic staff. The sister may also therefore have been in service and the postcard conjures up an interesting insight into a way of life where girls could correspond with each other as if they were part of the families they worked for.

The old Hillfoot road changes its name to Ochil Road at the bridge over Alva Burn, which is in the foreground of this view looking west along Beauclerc Street. In the left foreground is Bridge Cottage with the parapet of the bridge just beyond. The bridge later had an angled section built on to ease the corner into Brook Street, although this appears to have stood the test of time less well than the original structure. The cottage and the two-storey houses diagonally opposite have long gone; a fate that also appears imminent for the small works that occupied the sites on both sides of the road. The single-storey cottages in the background, on the south side of the road, are where Alva Academy is now. On a clear day – and the Hillfoots do occasionally have such things – the Wallace Monument can be seen in the distance from this viewpoint.

215481.J.V.

ALVA FROM THE HILL.

So steeply do the Ochils rise that people can get a good aerial view of the towns and villages below them without actually taking to the air – although many do, these days, with the aid of a hang-glider. In the centre of this view looking over the burgh from the hillside to the east of Alva Glen is the Strude or Boll Mill, a splendid six-storey structure erected about 1820. It is a plain building with a typically Georgian central pediment capped by a bell. This used to punctuate the day for Alva folk by being rung every morning and evening at six o'clock. The mill was, as the picture shows, part of a larger complex of buildings which were owned and operated by William Archibald & Son. Strude Mill stopped working in 1976, but was saved from demolition and converted into flats. It must be one of the finest surviving nineteenth century industrial buildings in Scotland.

STIRLING STREET, ALVA

Stirling Street, which is the name of the new Hillfoots road in Alva, is seen here in 1930. On the right is the Eadie Memorial Fountain, erected in 1889 to commemorate John Eadie, the son of a poor Alva family who became a professor of theology in Glasgow. The extension in front of the fountain is a horse trough, but when the road had to be widened to make room for a bus stance, not long after this picture was taken, the trough was disposed of and the fountain moved. Its new site was on the east side of the burn at the base of the MacArthur Braes. The shops behind the fountain are partially obscuring the Johnstone Arms, originally known as the Alva Inn. The turreted building re-forming the street line beyond it was built as the Liberal Club in 1901. The building in the foreground on the left is the Alva Glen Hotel.

Sir John Erskine originally intended Green Square (now called The Green) to be the centre of his planned town. He feued the north and west sides for development first with the north following the line of the old – and now demolished – street known as The Ark. Facing the camera on the left of this picture from 1905 is the old schoolhouse. It was later used as the Baptist Church and is the only building within this view still standing. Behind it, to the right, is James W. Stark's grocery. To its right, John Fowler's cabinet-maker's and upholsterer's shop was tacked onto the gable end of a house which was surrounded on three sides by The Green and Brook Street. The Green was always a busy shopping centre with, in later years, a tailor, cobbler, baker, ironmonger and shops where people could buy wool, sweeties, groceries or a bicycle. There was even a stable.

Alva railway station, seen here in 1909, was opened twice. The initial opening took place on 3 June 1863 when the first passenger train left for Stirling and Alloa while the second, 'official' opening, occurred three weeks later when James Johnstone had returned from London with his new wife Sarah Mary L'Estrange. James Johnstone was chairman of the company that had been set up two years earlier to build the short line. It ran from Cambus to Alva with only one intermediate station at Menstrie and Glenochil and one significant engineering structure, the bridge over the Devon east of Menstrie. Although James Johnstone was a prime mover in bringing the railway to Alva, he also gave it little chance to succeed commercially by refusing to allow it to cross his estate and continue east to Tillicoultry. The station closed in 1954.

The qualities usually associated with lovers' loans around the country were quietness, seclusion and a generally romantic setting, but while Alva's may have had some of these features it must have been at least unusual because it led to the cemetery. This grand tree-flanked entrance has now gone and the hedge-lined lane has been widened into the modern road called Lovers Loan. It is the very antithesis of romantic seclusion giving access not just to the expanded cemetery, but also to the modern housing that occupies the ground to the east and the slightly less modern homes tucked in behind the house on the left of the picture.

TILLICOULTRY

While the other Hillfoots towns can point proudly to a history coloured by grand castles or houses, Tillicoultry can claim even greater antiquity with an ancient fort on the hill known as Castle Craig on the west side of the burn.

Prior to the industrial expansion of the Hillfoots, Tillicoultry Parish consisted mainly of three little villages. Of these, Coalsnaughton, to the south of the Devon, developed as a mining community while the hamlets of Harviestoun and Ellistoun, known collectively as Eastertoun, or Easter Tillicoultry, were cleared in the nineteenth century to make way for improvements to Harviestoun estate. The third village, Westertoun, grew from being a small community nestling at the base of the glen into the burgh of Tillicoultry.

It was of course industry, and the woollen industry in particular, that brought about the change, although as early as the sixteenth century, long before the large-scale mills took over, Tillicoultry was producing wool cloth. Villagers, working on hand looms, made a heavy material known throughout the country as Tillicoultry serge. But the harnessing of the burn's power around 1800 transformed Tillicoultry's reputation. Instead of the coarse serge, the water-driven mills produced fine wool cloths, blankets, plaids and tartan shawls. They also encouraged a huge growth in Tillicoultry's population as, drawn by the promise of steady work and reasonable wages, large numbers of people were attracted to the burgh as it grew east and south along the burn and the new Hillfoots road.

While the hill burns initially provided the mills with water-power, this was replaced through the nineteenth century with steam power. Coal, the raw material needed to generate steam, was found in abundance in Clackmannanshire, and some of the county's most productive mines were just south of Tillicoultry over the Devon. Mining was not Tillicoultry's only extractive industry as the large scar made by the quarry on the hillside just below Castle Craig testifies. It was Tilly's industrial survivor, outlasting mining and woollen mills, although one of the mills, Devonvale, has found a new lease of life selling furniture and is once again making Tillicoultry a household name throughout Scotland.

Bridge and dam in Tillicoultry Glen.

Water Woes

Of all the flooding of all the burns that has occurred along the Ochils, that at Tillicoultry in August 1877 was arguably the worst. The burn flows out of hill bogs, but on 28 August 1877 these were unable to absorb a sudden torrential downpour, with disastrous results. Water burst off the hills as if a dam had failed. William Hutchison, the owner of the Castle Mill, and a mill girl, Isabella Miller, were drowned. They were on the bridge connecting the mill buildings on both sides of the burn when it was swept away. The torrent also tore up the roadways on either side of the burn and demolished buildings.

Tillicoultry Glen

Right of access to Tillicoultry's Mill Glen was acquired by the town council in 1926 and this wonderful asset was opened up for the townspeople with a path providing access onto the hills. The building of the path and bridges up the rocky cleft of the glen also created work at a time of high unemployment, three quarters of the wages bill being paid for by money from the Unemployed Grants Committee. As well as opening up the scenic grandeur of both hill and glen, the path also allowed people to see at close quarters some of delicate plants that inhabit the glen's damp and often sunless rock walls.

Tillicoultry Glen, with the quarry and Castle Craig to the left, is in the background of this view of the burnside from Upper Mill Street. The large mill building on the far bank was Robert Archibald's Middleton Mill, which started operations in 1805 and was expanded with new buildings in 1836, making it one of the largest in the burgh. It was latterly used by the Dunedin Stationery Company. At the head of the burn is the distinctive Clock Mill which was built in 1824 by a Borders wool manufacturer to make tartan shawls and other woollen goods. The mill building takes its name from the prominent clock on its south gable and is now used as a heritage and tourist information centre.

Upper Mill Street continues down the east side of the burn to where the new Hillfoots road is carried across the burn on a bridge built in 1895. The granite drinking fountain on the left was presented to the burgh in 1900 by Provost Walker on his retirement from council duties after 29 years' service. The Walker Fountain was one of four gifted to Tillicoultry which led to it being christened the 'Fountain Burgh'. Just across the bridge, out of picture to the left, was the east lodge of Alva House: the west lodge was situated just outside Alva and with the house and gardens occupying a commanding position midway between Alva and Tilly, and the grounds extending well beyond that, it was a property of considerable size. Somewhat less grand was the Royal Hotel in High Street, on the right of the picture.

The Royal, or Royal Arms, was one of three hotels grouped at the west end of High Street; the Castle Craig was opposite and the Crown further east on the north side of the street. They were Tillicoultry's main hostelries in the early twentieth century and their location in close proximity is a good indicator of the way that Tillicoultry grew. The town moved south along the burnside from its early beginnings at the foot of the glen and then east along the new road, or the High Street as it was known in Tilly. Most of the buildings were single-storey cottages or utilitarian shops with dwelling houses above. One such was Murray's bakery and confectioner's which offered its customers 'a good cup of tea' in its walled tea garden at the back of the premises, no doubt an attraction to those seeking an alternative to the strong drink on offer at the nearby hotels. The High Street was significantly altered in the 1960s when many of the buildings in this picture were demolished to make way for new housing.

The old Hillfoots road was virtually obliterated in some places where it crossed the Alva estate, but the line of it has survived at Tillicoultry. It crosses the burn on a small stone bridge which still exists beside a more modern structure. The road continues along Frederick Street (which can be seen in the distance on the left of this picture) and carries on across the top of the town as Walker Terrace (foreground). This was developed in the late nineteenth century with some fine Victorian villas lining the north side. One of the finest, at the east end of the terrace, was the Free Church manse which is now used as an architect's office. The large two-storey house in the centre of this picture is 'The Elms'. It is now separated from the single-storey villa to its right by Ochilview Road. This was put between them in the 1930s to give access to the remarkable Jamieson Gardens housing estate which was built in stages throughout that decade.

Stirling, Ochil, Hamilton and Hill Streets were built in the second half of the nineteenth century to provide mill-workers' housing. They run parallel with each other at an oblique angle between High Street and the old road comprising Walker Terrace and Frederick Street, which can be seen in the distance of this view of Stirling Street. This had two distinct sides with humbler-looking cottages along the west side (the left of this picture) and larger, better spaced out dwellings on the east side, where the Free Church was also built in 1844. The Church of Scotland Free was founded in 1843 when churchmen and churchgoers all over the country seceded from the established church in order to exercise more control over their places of worship. Free Church congregations often endured many years of temporary accommodation before being able to erect a new building, so the early date of Tilly's Free Church suggests that the town's seceders had sufficient money and influence to push ahead more quickly than others. Modern housing now occupies the site where the church stood.

'The Elms' in Walker Terrace can be seen at the far end of this picture of Ochil Street. At the northern end of the street was the Popular Institute, built in 1859. Twenty years after it was completed its distinctive tower, complete with clock and bell, was added. The tower was a gift from Captain James Archibald of the mill-owning family and its opening prompted a great celebration. A parade was followed by a concert at which an ode written in honour of the occasion was read, and the festivities were concluded with a firework display and illuminations. When the commercially-run institute got into financial difficulties in 1905 it was taken over by the town council and became the town hall. It was used as a cinema for many years, screening its first film in 1913 and its first talkie in 1931.

Tillicoultry from White Craigs.

2426.

Tillicoultry's shift south and east is graphically shown in this picture looking down from the hills. The planned streets of mill-workers' housing can be clearly seen on the left. As the mills grew through the mid-nineteenth century, the town prospered and mill workers were earning steady – and compared to the uncertain hand-to-mouth existence of the past – reasonably good money. They could afford to buy or rent better housing and were attracted to the cottages in these new streets. On the right are the mills lining the burnside with Middleton Mills in the foreground and Paton's Mills beyond. The gasworks can be seen behind Paton's Mills, with Tillicoultry School to its left. The school opened in 1876 with 600 pupils and was being used as a primary school when it was destroyed by fire in 1940 – an event which helps to date the picture as being from the 1930s or earlier. Devonvale Mills can be seen in the background with Devonside village to their right and Coalsnaughton in the distance.

The growth of Tillicoultry was further accelerated by the arrival of the railway. When the Stirling & Dunfermline Railway Company put forward proposals to link the two towns in 1845 they also included plans for a branch line from Cambus to Kinross. Their plan was to link up with the Edinburgh & Perth Direct Railway, but when that railway failed the Stirling & Dunfermline modified their plans and went ahead with a branch from Alloa to Tilly. It was opened to Glenfoot in 1851 and this remained a temporary terminus until the viaduct was built over the Devon and the line extended to the town. It was not taken on to Dollar and Kinross until the 1860s. The station was closed in 1964 only a year after its most prestigious passenger, Queen Elizabeth, stepped off a royal train on a tour of the area.

Buses started to appear in Tillicoultry towards the end of the First World War providing services to Stirling, Alloa and further afield. By the late 1920s the number of services had expanded considerably and Tilly had become a busy terminus as well being a stop on various through services. There were so many buses vying for space on the road that they presented a potential danger and so Provost Thomas Murray pressed the town council to provide a bus station – one of the first in Scotland. The new station is seen here in 1931 with a bus belonging to local operator Harper's who ran services between Tillicoultry and Alloa, and from Tillicoultry to Dunfermline by way of Dollar and Saline. If the volume of buses was as heavy as it was made out to be, then the boys with their 'bogie' or 'guider', made from a set of old pram wheels, were taking a risk playing where they could be run down – but maybe that was just part of the thrill!

ROSE GARDEN, TILLICOULTRY.

The distinctive clock at the east end of the bus station was donated by Provost Murray himself and in 1936 he also gifted the old men's shelter known as the 'Murray Howff', or the 'Square Parliament', where the town's elder statesmen could gather to set the world to rights. He also donated plants for the adjacent rock and rose gardens which provided a pleasant oasis beside the busy bus routes. Moss Road is in the background of this picture and the one of Murray Square on the facing page.

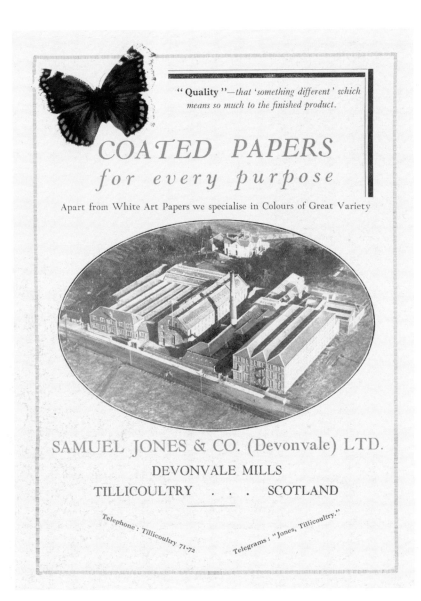

"**Quality**"—*that 'something different' which means so much to the finished product.*

COATED PAPERS
for every purpose

Apart from White Art Papers we specialise in Colours of Great Variety

SAMUEL JONES & CO. (Devonvale) LTD.

DEVONVALE MILLS

TILLICOULTRY . . . SCOTLAND

Telephone: Tillicoultry 71-72

Telegrams: "Jones, Tillicoultry."

The original Devonvale Mill was built as a woollen (tweed) mill in 1846 by J. & R. Archibald and expanded in the 1860s. It was used as a barracks during the First World War and after the war, in 1921, was taken over by the London paper-coating company of Samuel Jones & Co. Ltd. The manager was an energetic Londoner, Sydney Platfoot, under whose guidance the business prospered. He was always very attentive to employees' welfare and was responsible for building a number of employees' houses in Devonvale Crescent and Moss Road. He also provided the town with a much-needed new hall in 1940 when the Devonvale Hall was opened in Moss Road. Although Samuel Jones' employees had first call on the hall, the town was also allowed to use it for functions and concerts. Orlando and his Orchestra provided the entertainment on the first night and were followed over the years by many other famous entertainers. In 1964 Samuel Jones merged with Wiggins Teape who continued to operate at Devonvale until 1972. The old mill buildings are now used as a furniture warehouse.

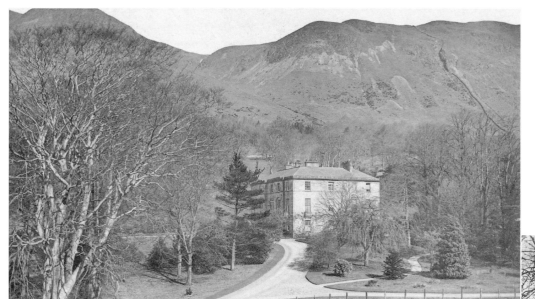

R. Wardlaw-Ramsay was the latest in a succession of owners when he bought Tillicoultry Estate in 1814. He built this fine house in 1829 to the east of Tilly itself. On his death in 1837 the estate, along with Whitehill Estate in Midlothian, passed to his son Robert Balfour Wardlaw-Ramsay. He immediately sold Tillicoultry House and part of the estate, but within three years had bought it back. It remained in the family until 1938 when it was abandoned and later demolished.

Situated further east, Harviestoun Castle was only a small mansion when John Tait acquired it in 1780 and began a process of improvement. His son Craufurd inherited the estate in 1800 and continued to effect improvements, but by 1822 had accrued heavy debts and attempted to sell it. He failed and so when he died in 1832 the Globe Insurance Company took over the property. They sold it in 1859 to Sir Andrew Orr, a former Lord Provost of Glasgow. He added further to the house, but by the early 1960s it had again fallen on hard times. Dollar Academy held preparatory school classes there in the early 1960s, but that was its last use. It was demolished with explosives in 1970.

HARVIESTOUN CASTLE, DOLLAR.

36718

DOLLAR

Dollar might have become a mill town like the other Hillfoots towns and villages. It grew up next to a fast-flowing burn which was used in the early nineteenth century to drive mills, but the last of them, the Brunt Mill beside the North Bridge, ceased to work in the 1830s. The loss of the mill was not the catastrophe it could have been because the future of Dollar had already been assured by a bequest made to the little parish in 1802 by a wealthy London merchant, John McNabb. He had left Dollar as a poor boy in 1745 and made his fortune in shipping, but the scale of his beneficence, and his vision of a charity or school for the poor of the parish, initially overwhelmed the 600 or so parishioners. Suggestions that the money should be used to build a poorhouse sparked rancorous disputes and court cases which were only resolved when the parish minister died in 1815 and was replaced by the Revd Andrew Mylne. Under his enlightened guidance the concept of a school took shape. It was founded in 1818 and was originally known as Dollar Institution, but in 1918 the name was altered to Dollar Academy, which became known as a fine educational establishment throughout the country, indeed the world.

The school influenced Dollar's development with a more spacious street layout than the other Hillfoots towns. Academy Place, a street of houses for teachers designed by the architect responsible for the school, set the tone for the other early nineteenth century streets. Dollar was not totally devoid of industry and with small mines along the Kelly Burn the genteel houses going up in the expanding burgh were not far from some run-down miners' cottages. Bleaching and quarrying were other industries, but Dollar was essentially a residential town. It continued to grow, with the area to the south of Bridge Street developed after the completion of the railway which gave Dollar easy access to all the major centres in Scotland.

The railway and coal continued to give Dollar an industrial purpose up to the 1970s, but the burgh itself remained focused on the Academy. Now the school, the motor car and proximity to the cities of the central belt have turned Dollar into a commuter town.

Water Woes

A few years after its opening, the railway was closed for some days when the same flood that did so much damage in Tillicoultry affected Dollar too. The burn tore off the hills in fearful spate and burst its banks below Sorley's Brae. It ripped up the East Burnside Road and caused the partial collapse of some houses. Further down, flood water swamped the railway and deposited a four foot pile of stones and debris on the tracks, including the smashed remnants of furniture from the damaged houses.

Looking down towards the burnside from Dollar's 'Old Town'.

OLD TOWN, DOLLAR

The old Hillfoots road still forms an integral part of Dollar. To the west, where it is flanked on the south side by the Academy and to the north by large private houses, it is known simply as the Back Road, but despite having to carry increased vehicular traffic it still retains some of the tree-lined appeal of the early twentieth century picture above. East of the burn it rises up the steep High Street of old Dollar seen (right) in a picture from the late nineteenth century. After the building of the new road and the Academy, the new town to the south grew apace while the little village became an isolated backwater. It was known, perhaps a little contemptuously, as the 'Old Town', its steep slopes and varied houses built at random angles with pantiled roofs contrasting sharply with the elegant conformity of the new Dollar.

Castle Campbell was the chief lowland stronghold of the Earls of Argyll, occupying a promontory with a commanding view over Dollar. Small burns on either side of the castle merge below it to become Dollar Burn. According to popular legend an imprisoned princess named the burns 'Care' and 'Sorrow' and also gave the castle its early name of 'Gloom'. This was dropped about 1490 in favour of Castle Campbell. The structure was begun in the fifteenth century and developed over the next 200 years, but it was set on fire in the mid-seventeenth century – the date is believed to have been 1654 and the likely culprits were General Monk's Cromwellian troops. The castle was in a ruinous state in 1948 when Mr J. E. Kerr of Harviestoun offered to gift it, along with Dollar Glen, to the National Trust for Scotland. The trust could only take on such onerous responsibilities if the Ministry of Works – the predecessor of Historic Scotland – was prepared to enter into a guardianship agreement to care for the castle. Local people were also, in effect, challenged to raise funds to restore and maintain the paths and bridges in the glen. They did, and with the future of both castle and glen secured the trust accepted the gifts in 1950.

The nursery, on the left of this picture of the West Burnside in the 1880s, continued in operation until just before the Second World War when a number of houses were built on its ground. The Academy preparatory school was built between them and the main school at the same time. The area had begun to change some time before that, however, with the golf course clubhouse being built on the site of the small cottage half-hidden behind the wall in the centre of the picture. The course was developed at the beginning of the twentieth century at a time when Dollar aspired to be an inland holiday resort, and the lack of a decent golf course was seen as a serious drawback. A company was formed, the hillside site selected and on a bright September day in 1906 the Countess of Mar and Kellie drove the first ball. She continued round the course and was presented with a driver as a memento of the occasion. The new course appears to have achieved its objective, as this verse from a poem in the *Alloa Journal* of 1909 suggests:

> If you claim to be a golfer and delight to tread the green
> A better course than Dollar has we're sure you've never seen.
> The approaches are magnificent, the bunkers most sublime,
> You will never tire of golfing 'till the other end of time,
> At Dollar.

The differences between the old and new towns of Dollar are clear from this 1930s view of the burgh taken from the tower of the Parish Church. The Burnsides intersect at right angles with Bridge Street which runs straight and true through the town centre. In the foreground is Woodville, my childhood home. The building opposite was where the Robertson brothers (I think they were brothers) ran a joinery business – one of them was named Guthrie and got quite a shock when he was in our house one day. He had rarely encountered anyone else with the same name and when my mother lost patience with me, he thought she was shouting at him until the misunderstanding was explained. He laughed, she laughed, and I got away with whatever mischief I had been up to! Beside the Robertsons' was the Clydesdale and North of Scotland Bank – now the Clydesdale.

Dollar and the Ochil Hills.

2527.

This view across the town was taken from the same vantage point as the picture on the previous page and almost certainly at the same time. Dominating the foreground is the former United Presbyterian Church which saw worship from the 1870s to 1910 when the congregation amalgamated with the West Free Church. After that it became the church hall for the Parish Church, then a dining hall for the Academy and latterly a church hall again known as the East Burnside Hall. To its right are the old parish schoolhouse built in 1780 and to the right of that the ruins of the old Parish Church which dates from 1775. In the background, beyond the churches, school and burnside is the Academy.

William Playfair, one of the finest architects of his time, was invited to design the school and Mr Beattie of Edinburgh was engaged as the contractor. The foundation stone was laid on 30 April 1819 and the elegant and distinctive buildings were completed by 1822/3. The Revd Andrew Mylne established the mix of pupils. He determined that schooling was to be offered to the poor as a right and to the rich as a privilege to be paid for. Pupils from outside the parish would be encouraged to attend as boarders to influence the manners and work of the village children. Over the years those children mixed with colleagues from a wide variety of backgrounds and from all over the world – one of the Academy's curious traditions was to arrange sporting competitions between pupils selected on the basis of being Britishers or foreigners. These included children who, although of British nationality, were born overseas. Hockey was the principal winter sport for the girls, regardless of nationality!

Tennis was the girls' summer sport although not always on these courts. Over the years there have been many changes and additions to the buildings and facilities. The science and domestic building was added in 1910, the sports ground in 1920 and the preparatory school in 1937. But the most dramatic change was unplanned and unwanted: on the morning of Friday 24 February 1961 the main Playfair building went on fire. Eleven fire appliances converged on the school and pupils threw a dam across the burn to provide them with a head of water, but despite all their efforts the interior was destroyed; the clock on the facade stopped at 6.52 a.m. The library of 12,000 books was lost along with sports trophies and artefacts gifted by former pupils from around the world. Fortunately the shell of the building survived and rebuilding within it began in October 1962, but within a few months fire returned to haunt the Academy when the preparatory school went up in flames. With these setbacks behind it, the school's response to pressures for change in the 1980s was to become independent, and while this preserved much of its unique character, the socially inclusive link with the townspeople was sadly lost.

After the First World War, Dollar Academy erected a memorial to commemorate the former pupils and men from the town who had died. It was completed in 1921 to the designs of the sculptor and former pupil George Paulin. Nearly 30 years later, after the Second World War, he was asked to design another memorial which forms the centrepiece of this Garden of Remembrance on the corner of Devon Road and Bridge Street. Tucked in behind the trees on the left is the West Church. It was built for the Free Church congregation in 1859, and continued as a place of worship for the Church of Scotland when the Free Church reunited with it in 1929. When the congregations of the West and Parish Churches amalgamated in 1975 the building was converted into housing. Further west, at the junction of Harviestoun Road with Mylne Avenue, was the Scottish Episcopal Church of St James the Great, completed in 1882.

It is a melancholy thought that the second global conflict marked by the Garden of Remembrance may have claimed the lives of some of these boys from the Academy's Officer Training Corps. They are on a church parade in the early 1930s and are lined up for inspection outside the West Church. At this point Bridge Street becomes Harviestoun Road, and just to the east of the church Devon Road runs south to the bridge over the Devon at the Rackmill. At the Bridge Street/Devon Road T-junction the milestone (there may also have been a sign) used to proclaim that Stirling, Dunfermline and Milnathort were each twelve miles away. It made Dollar feel like the centre of the known universe. Nowadays the milestone is unpainted and the signs are more accurate and less fun. The picture looks east along Bridge Street towards the Parish Church.

The bell tower of the Parish Church, from where the pictures on pages 40 and 41 were taken, is in the centre background of this view looking east along Bridge Street to the South Bridge. The church was built in 1841 to the designs of London architect William Tite. To the right, in front of the trees, is the clock erected in 1912 as a memorial to Dr William Spence, the town's doctor for over 23 years and someone who was sorely missed when he died following a motor accident. On the left is Muckersie's, the stationers, where some of the old picture postcards featured in this book may have been bought, although this one was produced for the Workers' Travel Association, which took over the grand mansion of Dollarbeg, south of the Devon, in the 1920s and formally opened it as a hostel-cum-hotel in 1934. John Muckersie was on the town council for many years and served as provost of Dollar from 1956 to 1962.

This picture postcard of Station Road, looking north past its junction with Dewar Street, was indeed bought from Muckersie's shop. Station Road was, like other streets to the south of Bridge Street, developed in the second half of the nineteenth century after the arrival of the railway. The continuation of the railway from Tillicoultry to Kinross was authorised by Parliament in 1858. The Kinross to Rumbling Bridge section was built first, but work on the Tilly to Rumbling Bridge section was not started until 1867. The original idea was to complete the whole section before opening any of it, but the plan was changed and the line opened to Dollar in April 1869. There was no special train; the 11.15 a.m. from Alloa to Tillicoultry just carried on to Dollar, but there was a celebration when it arrived.

Dollar and the Ochil Hills from the South. 2532.

The Devon Valley line settled into a routine of passenger services, and although coal had been mined at Dollar for many years it generated little if any traffic. All that changed in the early 1940s when the Alloa Coal Company opened Dollar mine at West Pitgober. It was a short-lived affair lasting only until 1953, but the National Coal Board reopened it in 1957 and this time the railway really came into its own, carrying special coal trains direct from the mine to the new Kincardine power station. There was a special passenger train in June 1963 when Her Majesty, Queen Elizabeth left Dollar station for Tillicoultry after opening the rebuilt Academy following the fire. The exalted status of having been trod by royal feet did nothing to save the station which was closed the following year, although the line from Alloa to Dollar mine remained open until 1973 when the mine closed. The picture shows the embankment and viaduct over the Devon to the east of Dollar.